MIGHTY OAK
TEST PREP

Guide to Mastering the NEW (2016) ACT Essay

by Shane Burnett and Kristin Leeson

ACT is a registered trademark of ACT, Inc, which was not involved with the production of, and does not endorse, this product.

Foreword

We (the tutors at Mighty Oak) were excited when we heard that the ACT was going to be replacing its old essay with a new, improved version starting in September of 2015. The new version looked like it had several improvements over the old essay – more time to plan, more time to write, and a three-perspective approach that acknowledged that issues aren't necessarily black-and-white.

When the news came out, we had expected that ACT would update its official test-preparation book ("The Real ACT Prep Guide", an excellent source of practice material) in the summer of 2015 to reflect these changes to the test. However, summer came and went, and the fall testing season arrived with no changes to the book.

More than three months after the introduction of the new-style essay, a new edition of the Real ACT Prep Guide finally arrived. Hooray! Taking three months to update the only official ACT prep book isn't exactly speedy, but better late than never, right? Unfortunately, the updated version of the book (released on Jan 20, 2016) changed only the cover art and the publisher. Not one of the practice tests inside was updated to reflect the new essay format. What's worse, the book still includes a chapter of advice for the old-style essay, which is sure to confuse and mislead unsuspecting students.

We are confident that an updated "Real ACT Prep Guide" that includes the new essay will eventually arrive. Until then, however, we have created this essay guide to help students excel.

Thank you to our world-class co-teachers Rose Paik and Johan Michalove and to all of our terrific students, past and present. Also, a big thank you to our not-so-exemplary students (you know who you are) because we learned even more from you. Each tutoring relationship, for nearly twenty years, has been meritorious, and we love our Seattle practice.

--Kristin and Shane
February 2016

Shane Burnett and Kristin Leeson (aka Mighty Oak Test Prep) have more than 30 years of combined experience helping students to prepare for the SAT, ACT, and other standardized tests. Their home base is in Seattle, WA, where they not only teach to the tests, but can be found some Saturday mornings taking the real tests, too.

Introduction

We know that your time is valuable, so we'll keep this book (and this introduction) concise. If you're like our tutoring students, you want three things:

+ You want to know what to expect on test day
+ You want to know how to get a great score
+ You want lots of practice materials

We're here to help.

For the multiple-choice parts of the test, The Real ACT Prep Guide (Third Edition), published by the makers of the ACT, is the best book you can use to prepare for the test. If you master the multiple-choice content of the five real formerly-administered ACTs included in the book, you'll get a great score and there should be no surprises on test day. However, the book has one huge problem:

The ACT revamped its its Writing Test (essay) in September 2015 and has not yet updated its Prep Guide to reflect this change. In fact, the book contains misinformation. The entire section on the Writing Test (pages 120-144) is WRONG. It refers to the former essay format, which is no longer used.

IGNORE PAGES 120-144 OF THE THIRD EDITION OF THE REAL ACT PREP GUIDE. THE INFORMATION IS OBSOLETE, INACCURATE, AND MISLEADING.

You should also ignore the Practice Writing Test Prompts at the end of each of the five practice tests in the book. Again -- wrong format, wrong pacing.

To help you get a great essay score, we have written this concise guide. Our approach begins with a "Big Picture" essay strategy, which is enough guidance for some students, and continues with a "Cheat Sheet" approach for those who need even more specific help.

To ensure you have plenty of opportunities to practice, the last part of the book includes a dozen mock essay prompts and one copy of the essay sheets where you'll write your essays. You can tear out the sheets and make copies or go to mightyoaktestprep.com/downloads.htm to download printable pdfs.

Frequently Asked Questions

Where does the essay appear? How much time? How many pages?

The NEW ACT Writing Test (effective September 2015) is a 40-minute essay that's administered as an "optional" extra 5th section after you complete the four multiple-choice sections of the test. You will have one page to plan your essay and four pages to write it (with a wooden #2 pencil -- no mechanical pencil, no pen, no keyboard). You will be presented with a topic and three perspectives on that topic. Your task is to plan and write an essay that develops your perspective on the issue and persuasively explains why your position is the best one. Your overall Writing Test Score (now on a 36-point scale) will be based on 4 sub-scores that the graders give you. This may sound more challenging than the old 2-position, 30-minute, 12-point essays that are in the Real ACT Prep Guide, but we actually prefer the new format.

I've heard that the essay is optional. True?

Not really. It's optional in the same way that the SAT Subject Tests are optional -- or the ACT itself, for that matter, in that **it's up to the colleges** to decide whether they require you to submit the version of the ACT with the essay or not. As I write this (January, 2016), many colleges are still on the fence about the new essay. Some (Harvard, Yale, Princeton) have announced that they want it. Others (Penn, Cornell, Columbia) have announced that they don't. Many are still dealing with the mountain of applications they've just received from seniors and haven't yet made any announcements about whether they will require the essay or not. Even if every college has announced their requirements for the class of 2015, it boils down to this: most students will take the ACT for the first time when they are juniors, but won't finalize their college lists or start submitting applications until they are seniors. Play it safe and take the test with the essay.

True story: one of our students has a friend who scored a 99th-percentile 33 on his ACT. Excellent! Unfortunately, he took the version without the essay and has since learned that his top choice school requires it. He needs to retake the whole test, and he's not confident that he'll be able to match his first score.

How is the essay scored?

The new essay is on the same familiar 36-point scale as the other sections of the ACT. This score is the result of 4 subscores -- what we think of as the "IDOL" scoring system. You will receive a score between 2 and 12 on each of these 4 categories:

I: IDEAS AND ANALYSIS
D: DEVELOPMENT AND SUPPORT
O: ORGANIZATION
L: LANGUAGE & GRAMMAR

(we'll talk about how to maximize your score on all 4 of these areas in the next chapter.)

Your total score on these 4 sub-sections will range from 8 to 48. As with all the multiple-choice sections, this number is then converted to the traditional 36-point scale.

Because the essay is technically optional, <u>it is not a factor in your composite score</u>. If you get a 36 on the multiple-choice portion of the test, but fall asleep for the essay, you'll still get a 36 composite score on your ACT.

The ACT score report also includes an "ELA" (English Language Arts) score. This is another 36-point score and is a weighted average that combines your performance on the multiple-choice English section with your essay performance.

How do colleges use the essay?

Each college chooses how it uses the essay. Many don't use it at all. Some treat it as an equally-weighted 5th section of the test, or use another formula to integrate it into your composite ACT score. Some universities tell us "the essay is the most valuable part of standardized testing." Colleges also have access to a scanned copy of your essay, so they can read the whole thing if they'd like. Some colleges have reported that they use the essay not for its score, but as a "validity check" for the personal statement you submit with your application. Check the school websites (or ask an admissions officer or your college counselor) if you want specific details about how the essay will be used at the schools to which you intend to apply.

Who scores the essay?

Two separate graders, each of whom sees a scan of your essay on his/her computer screen. Each grader has only a couple of minutes to read your essay and give it four scores (the "IDOL" system mentioned above), each on a 1-6 point scale. The 2 readers' scores are then combined to create the 2-12 point subscores you'll see on your score report. If the two graders disagree by more than one point on any of the scores, the essay goes to a tie-breaker master grader to determine the score your essay deserves.

How legible does my writing need to be?

NEATNESS IS IMPORTANT -- graders won't penalize you for messy writing, but if they can't read what you have written, then they can't give your essay the score it deserves. The scanners are very sensitive (to ensure they pick up every nuance of your number-2-penciled thoughts), which means they often pick up stray marks and the "ghosts" of words you have erased, no matter how carefully and thoroughly you erase them. Words written over erased words are often illegible. If you make a mistake, ~~cross out~~ the word or phrase and write beside it. If there's no space, write an asterisk ("*") and put the correction at the bottom of the page. Neatness makes it easy for the graders to analyze your essay and give you a great score.

Can I use a mechanical pencil or a pen?

No. You must use a traditional wooden #2 hardness (also known as "HB") pencil. No mechanical pencils, no pens, no computer keyboard. ACT is keeping it "old school". And by the end of 40 minutes, your hand will probably hurt.

What is a typical essay question?

It's difficult to say what the "typical" essay is about (because the new essay has only been offered a few times), but it is clear that the scope of the questions is broader than it was with the old-style ACT essay (which typically focused on issues affecting high-schoolers). The two officially-released essay prompts ask about conflicts between public health and personal freedom, or about the mixed blessings that computers and robots have brought to our society. Common sense says that they will attempt to include issues of broad relevance (diligence, creativity, freedom, education, progress) without wading into overtly political topics (gun control, reproductive issues).

Can I see the essay prompt at the beginning of the test so I can have more time to think about it?

No. First, that would be against the rules. The essay is attempting to measure what you're capable of doing under tight time pressure, so peeking at the essay prompt at the beginning of the test would give you an unfair advantage. Second, the essay is in a separate sealed test packet that isn't handed out until the multiple-choice part of the test is completed and turned in. Nice try, though.

Isn't it true that longer essays get higher scores?

Don't confuse correlation with causation. Essays that get the highest scores are often ones that fill up most of the space, but that's because these "perfect 36" essays are stuffed with great examples, stellar vocabulary, and scintillating style. If you are confident that a long essay automatically gets you a high score, your job is simple: just write "I'm awesome!" over and over until you fill all four pages. Let's see the score your "essay" receives.

Longer essays make a better initial impression than shorter essays do, but to get the best possible score, the essay needs to be long because it's filled with well thought-out ideas, not just because it has a lot of words.

So how long does the essay need to be?

Long enough to impress the graders. Back when students only had 30 minutes to complete the assignment, the great essays tended to be 2 1/2 to 3 pages long. Now that you're getting more time and more perspectives to analyze, we recommend completely filling three pages and having at least a little bit on the fourth page.

Can I write in the first person?

Yes. In fact, for the ACT essay, I recommend it. Many high school students tell me that their teachers will not let them use the first person voice (using the word "I") in their essays at school, and they are afraid to do so on the ACT essay. Your job is to develop a position and support your ideas with examples. You will be sharing YOUR opinion with YOUR examples, which are often personal ones. It would be very difficult to do this without using the first person.

Section 1: How To Master the Essay

As mentioned before, you'll get 40 minutes and four pages (plus a page for outlining/planning) to write your essay. The prompt will introduce a topic and then share three perspectives on that topic. Your job is to develop a position and convincingly argue that position, analyzing the strengths and weaknesses of each perspective.

Here's an example:

Standardized Testing

As the number of students applying to colleges increases, and the average number of applications submitted by each student also increases, colleges face an increasingly difficult task each year in deciding which students will be admitted. A major tool used by colleges is the use of standardized tests like the ACT, which give schools a quick, uniform way to compare one student to another. However, detractors assert that colleges place far too much emphasis on these standardized test results, arguing that the tests measure a limited set of skills under unrealistic circumstances.

Read and carefully consider these perspectives. Each suggests a particular way of thinking about the role of standardized testing in college admissions.

Perspective One	Perspective Two	Perspective Three
Standardized tests give colleges an efficient, consistent "apples to apples" method to compare applicants. By preparing for these tests, students also demonstrate to colleges that they have the discipline to master a subject.	ACT scores can be useful when considering an applicant, but GPA, personal statement, letters of recommendation, and resume are more important factors for schools to consider.	A number of prestigious colleges have now chosen to adopt "test optional" admissions policies, and many of these schools have reported that their students without test scores are every bit as good as those with test scores.

Essay Task

Write a coherent, unified essay in which you evaluate multiple perspectives given on the best use of standardized tests in admissions. In your essay, be sure to:

--analyze and evaluate the perspectives given
--state and develop your own perspective on the issue
--explain the relationship between your perspective and those given

Your perspective may be in full agreement with any of the others, in partial agreement, or wholly different. Whatever the case, support your ideas with logical reasoning and detailed, persuasive examples.

The Big Picture

Your score is derived from four sub-scores, each of which are weighted equally:

Ideas & Analysis -- how carefully have you considered the argument and the three perspectives?
Development & Support -- can you convincingly expand on the perspectives?
Organization -- does your essay flow logically?
Language -- are you writing like someone who is ready for college?

You have 40 minutes to write this essay -- that's 10 minutes (33%) more time than students were given on the old essay, but you still get the same number of pages (4) as before. Use 5-10 of these minutes to PLAN your essay. Really. When we gave a free proctored exam, we found that most students were so worried about the clock that they started writing the essay right away. These students overwhelmingly ran out of ideas before they ran out of either time or space. In a perfect world, you want to be putting the final period on the last sentence in your concluding paragraph at the bottom of the fourth page at the exact moment that the proctor says "Time's up". If you do not devote your first several minutes to planning your essay, you will have a very hard time writing an essay with the depth of analysis, quality of examples, and organization that ACT expects. Ideas, Development, and Organization are ¾ of your grade -- the thinking and planning you do during this first five minutes pave the way for the next 35 minutes. <u>Plan well, and the essay more or less writes itself</u>.

Consider the Conflict

At the heart of each essay prompt is a conflict -- the conflict between the ways that computers have improved our lives and have simultaneously taken away some elements of human interaction, or the conflict between the rights of the individual and the rights of the community, for example. Be sure you understand the central conflict -- re-read the prompt, if necessary. If your essay doesn't really address the topic, it will be harder for the graders to give you a good score.

In the sample essay, the main conflict is whether relying on ACT scores is a good way or bad way to judge college applicants. Build your essay from this conflict.

Make a T-chart

A T-chart is a simple way to organize your ideas -- the "pros" and "cons" of the argument. This is where you Develop those Ideas. Dig deep. Be creative. Look at the specific points made in the essay prompt and the three perspectives and write them down on your chart.. Think about how this issue has affected you or your friends. Think about any relevant news stories you may have heard. Think about anything from English or History class that may be relevant. Use your imagination and dream up some scenarios. Make stuff up? Yes, but be reasonable.

Your T-chart should look something like the one below. You can start by filling it in with examples from the prompt, and then start brainstorming. Are there good arguments to counter the ones you've already written? Put them in the other column. Try to think about all three perspectives. After you fill in the arguments already in the prompts (and any counterarguments), start brainstorming additional arguments. Can you think of any? Here are some ideas to start with -- feel free to add more.

Standardized tests GOOD	Standardized tests BAD
--same test worldwide, so easy apples-to-apples comparison of students	--everyone may be judged on the same scale, but that's irrelevant if the tests don't measure skills needed for college
--mastering the content of the test shows colleges that you have persistence and tenacity, and it's good practice for the numerous tests you will be taking in college, too	--it's much more useful to master the content of something you'll actually use later in life than to master standardized testing
--how do test-optional schools define a "good" student? If they are not measuring their applicants quantitatively, then simply saying students are "as good" is a subjective measurement that's hard to verify	--test-optional schools say the quality of students is the same when ACT is not a factor in admissions

If you're having trouble coming up with good ideas, I'd like you to....

Meet my friend "Al"

...think about all those words that end in "-al" -- "FinanciAL", "SocietAL", "PhysicAL", "HistoricAL, CulturAL, IntellectuAL, PersonAL, etc).

Is there a financial argument to be made here? Of course there is. You know that some students spend thousands of dollars on test prep classes to increase their scores. Is that fair? On the other hand, you also know that plenty of students get 99th percentile scores by preparing on their own. In this case, the ACT can be seen as a low-cost opportunity to compete with those students whose families pay to plump up résumés with epic safaris to Africa.

Is there a societal argument? Indeed. Critics of standardized testing have long argued that the vocabulary, reading passages, math examples, and other content in the test are geared toward a specific socioeconomic group ("rich white guys"), which could help certain groups and make high scores harder for others.

Can we consider a historical perspective? Sure. A Political one? Yes. A cultural one? Check. Pick aspects of the argument that you think are relevant and that you know something about (or can imagine.)

Pick a Position

ACT provides three perspectives on the issue. Typically, the three perspectives span the spectrum -- if it's a political prompt, for example, one perspective will likely take a very liberal view, another will likely take a very conservative view, and the third will likely fall somewhere in the middle. Figure out which position is closest to your own (if you already have a position) or which position sounds most reasonable to you. It's usually easiest to write from a perspective you actually believe. Note that you don't need to entirely agree with any of the perspectives.

Look at the sample essay prompt (about standardized testing) and consider how you feel about the issue. Perspective 1 sounds like it was written by a testing company, Perspective 2 is pretty balanced, and Perspective 3 sounds like it was written by someone bitter who got a very bad score on the test. You're preparing yourself for the ACT right now, so you probably don't really believe Position 3, and you probably also believe that everything you have been doing in school should count, so Position 2 is likely the easiest perspective to write "from the heart". You can also pick a position that doesn't fit neatly into one of the three columns -- you could consider yourself a "Position 2.5" if there are aspects of Two and Three that you like.

Start Writing

With all of your main points thought out and scribbled down, you're ready to begin. You should have 30-35 minutes left, so plan to spend around 6-7 minutes per paragraph. Here are a few pointers to keep in mind as you write:

--Keep in mind that your score is composed of 4 sub-scores: Ideas & Analysis, Development & Support, Organization, and Language.

--Some people choose to write about the *topic* described the essay prompt, and some choose to analyze the *essay prompt* itself. In other words, some people say "Advocates of standardized tests argue...." and "Ultimately, the use of the ACT in college admissions...." while others say "Perspective 1 argues..." and "The prompt asserts that..." The choice is yours: whether you write about the topic or analyze the piece of paper that the ACT has given you about the topic, ether approach can get you a perfect score.

--Try to <u>stay inside the box</u> on your lined pages. If your words creep outside the boxes, it's possible that they won't be picked up by the scanner.

--Be sure your first paragraph introduces the topic, includes (at least briefly) the perspectives provided by the ACT, and lets the reader know your perspective (in the form of your <u>thesis</u>) or tells the reader that it's a complicated issue and that your essay will be exploring these perspectives.

--Plan to write <u>three body paragraphs</u>, using either the 3 perspectives they already provide you (in the three boxes) or with 3 "-al"s (financial, ethical, societal, etc) -- or a mix of the two.

--The "boxes" approach considers each of the three perspectives (the ones the ACT puts in the boxes on the essay prompt page) separately. Using this approach, each body paragraph considers one of the boxed perspectives and its strengths and weaknesses. Starting with the two perspectives you disagree with and concluding with the perspective you agree with is often the most powerful way to arrange the body paragraphs using this approach, though you can also lead with your favorite and then tear apart the other two perspectives in the subsequent paragraphs. The "boxes" approach works best when you really agree with one of the three perspectives (and aren't stuck between two perspectives). It's also often the easier approach if you don't love the topic or are tired out from the prior 4 sections,.

--The "-al" approach organizes the essay by the "-al" topics you brainstormed in the T-chart. For example, if you believe that the financial perspective is most important, your first paragraph should discuss the issue from a financial point of view, analyzing the strengths and weaknesses of the boxed perspectives when it's appropriate. The next paragraph could tackle the issue from a ethical perspective, from a societal perspective, etc.

--Build your argument with convincing examples that support your perspective. Specific examples ("When my brother's ACT score kept him from getting into Stanford") are more compelling than hypothetical examples ("if someone were to be rejected from his or her dream school"). Studies and reports are also compelling: "a report from Lewis and Clark concluded that its students who applied without standardized test scores had college GPAs identical to those who submitted scores.") If you don't remember exactly which university or newspaper published a study, don't worry -- the graders are not fact-checking.

--When you're finishing your second body paragraph, check the time. You should have roughly 14 minutes left. If you have not managed your time well and have less time than expected, make your third body paragraph brief -- or eliminate it altogether. If, on the other hand, you find yourself ahead of schedule, you can consider adding an additional body paragraph with another "al".

--When you've completed your body paragraphs, it's time to wrap up your essay with a conclusion. Finish by summarizing the points you made in your body paragraph, emphasizing which perspective is best, and potentially tie it back in to your introduction or wrap things up with a big bang.

--If you have any time left over at the end, go back and review what you've written. Remember that the machines that will be scanning your essay are set to be very sensitive. In an attempt to ensure that every pencil stroke is captured, the machines often pick up stray marks, poorly-erased words, and even well-erased words. Words written over erased words are often very hard for graders to read, so be sure to erase very thoroughly, or if possible, just ~~cross out the word or phrase~~ and write in your new words above the crossed-out word or on a new line. You can also make an asterisk (*) and then tack on the phrase at the bottom of the page or at the end of the essay.

If you feel like you're already pretty good at writing essays in school and/or enjoy writing, then these instructions should give you enough information to put together a "perfect 36" essay. We have included a sample essay that incorporates many of these ideas on the next several pages. It's not flawless (the graders don't expect perfection from a handwritten 40-minute essay) but it should give you a good idea of what ACT likes to see.

(Yes, the first page of the essay does really start a couple of inches down from the top. On the real test, this is where you put your name, test number, etc. These sheets accurately represent the amount of space you will have on test day.)

Start the WRITING TEST here.

Every year, more than a million high school students submit applications to colleges and universities around the world. Anxious teens toil for months to ensure every facet of the application is perfect -- personal statements and resumes are polished until they shine. Yet the one component that often takes the greatest time to achieve is the one that takes up the least space -- the student's standardized test score. To colleges, the benefits of standardized tests like the SAT and ACT are easy to see -- students are all graded by the same criteria on a uniform scale, making it quick and simple to compare one student to another. Critics argue, however, that schools should not put too much stock in these scores. They assert that the tests don't measure skills that are relevant to college, that the wealthy have unfair advantages in preparing for the tests, and that the scores have little value in predicting college success. Because standardized test scores provide such a quick and easy way to compare students, they often play a significant role in the admissions decision. However, I believe that these tests have enough problems that they

If you are not done, please continue on the next page.

WRITING TEST

should be used only as a secondary factor, behind more relevant criteria like GPA.

Some of the problems with the SAT and ACT become clear when we view the issue from a financial perspective. Test supporters assert that the exams are inherently fair because every student takes the same test. Though the test may be the same for every student, preparation for the test is not. Most students from low-income areas march into the test center with little or no preparation, whereas students from middle- and upper-class families often devote substantial time and money to test preparation courses and tutoring. In addition, some argue that the content of the test itself demonstrates socioeconomic bias. If the test includes a reading passage about lacrosse, a crew regatta, or a visit to Washington DC, who's most likely to already have the most familiarity with the topic? It should come as no surprise, then, to learn that SAT and ACT scores are more closely correlated with family income than with GPA or other academic factors.

Of course, completely ignoring standardized test scores comes with its own problems. Grade point averages, though ostensibly on a common scale just like the ACT, can vary widely from state to state, from district to district, and even from teacher to teacher. We all know that some

If you are not done, please continue on the next page.

WRITING TEST

schools have reputations for handing out 4.0s to anyone with a pulse. Over the past few years, my hometown newspaper has reported on several grade-related scandals. In one, the school principal was caught inflating students' grades to give the appearance that the school was academically improving; in another, a high school was letting students replace sub-par grades on their transcripts with new grades obtained from for-profit online classes. In this environment, it's clear that relying solely on GPA is a dangerous proposition.

Offering students the opportunity to apply to college without submitting test scores is an option that has been gaining traction recently. However, this approach is also not free of problems. One issue is that, fairly or not, many schools that don't require scores are simply viewed as being less prestigious than those that do. Another problem is practical in nature: reading ACT scores is quick and easy, but evaluating a student more meaningfully is time-consuming and expensive. Both Harvard and Stanford had nearly 40,000 applications last year; meaningfully assessing each of these students without the benefit of standardized test scores would be a Herculean, onerously expensive task.

I believe that the best approach to the use of ACT scores in college admissions is a hybrid one. Test scores, in com-

If you are not done, please continue on the next page.

WRITING TEST

bination with other quantitative metrics like GPA, should be used to "thin out the herd" of applicants, and once the stack of applications reaches a reasonable size, a more qualitative, hands-on, in-depth approach should be used. Most of us know someone who, despite having a dazzling personality, a rock-solid work ethic, an admirable GPA, and a mile-long resume of noteworthy extracurriculars, still has a crummy ACT score. For these students who are competitive in every way but ACT, there should be some alternate application method that discounts test scores. After all, I believe that colleges, students, and the standardized test companies share a common goal: to ensure that each college is able to identify and assemble the best possible student body as efficiently as possible.

> *Notes: A very strong essay overall. The introductory paragraph is pretty long, but it's demonstrating to the graders that the writer really understands the complexities of the topic. There's lots of good college-level vocabulary and usage -- "Anxious teens toil for months," rather than "High-schoolers work hard," for example. "criteria", "secondary factor", "demonstrates", "ostensibly", "gaining traction". As for the body paragraphs, the essay is a hybrid. The first body paragraph is an "-al" ("financial"), the 2nd is a critique of Perspective 3, and the 3rd paragraph is back to "-al" (logistical? practical?) The conclusion makes the writer's position crystal clear and wraps up the essay nicely.*

Feel like you're ready to start crafting masterful essays?
Flip to the practice essay prompts that start on page 22.

Still not confident that you can craft a "36" essay?
Have no fear -- flip the page and learn about the Cheat Sheet.

STOP the Writing Test.

The Cheat Sheet:
a (nearly) painless template for crafting a high-scoring essay

One of the most successful parts of our "wrap-up" lessons with our tutoring students the week before the real test is the making of "cheat sheets" where all the key points are summarized onto a clear, simple page.

Before we go any farther, let's be perfectly clear: there is no single "right way" or "magic formula" for writing the essay. Ultimately, the ACT wants to see your ability to analyze an issue and then write clearly and persuasively at a collegiate level. The "IDOL" (Ideas, Development, Organization, Language/Grammar) scale shows the four primary areas that you need to master to get a perfect score. As long as you have covered those four bases, the scoring system provides you with a lot of wiggle-room to craft an essay using your own style, emphasizing your own strengths, and writing with your own voice.

However, many of our students find the prospect of four blank pages and 40 minutes of time to be overwhelming and terrifying. For those students, we have developed this framework to consistently craft a "fill in the blanks" high-scoring essay.

In a couple of pages, you'll see the form itself with the main reminders of what is essential for your best essay. On test day, the ACT will give you a full page of scratch paper to plan your essay -- but that is just a blank page. For now, let's start with this template where you simply have some blanks to fill in. We will customize this cheat sheet together. You can tear the page out of this booklet and make copies (or print copies at mightyoaktestprep.com/downloads.htm), and then let's pick an essay -- any one of the 12 topics here in this book -- and fill out the key parts of the form. Once you get used to filling in the blanks, you should have no problem writing down the relevant info on the blank "planning" sheet at the actual test.

If you have gotten this far in our book, we hope you've realized that all good standardized essays have a sort of formula. Does this mean that they all are identical ? No. Let's say we're baking chocolate chip cookies. There are key ingredients that must be present to make sure our creation bakes into...well....cookies. There are must-have elements in baking so that the chemistry works every time. Similarly, there are also must-have elements in writing to craft a high-scoring essay every time. But there are also places in any recipe where you can improvise and embellish, by adding oats, more vanilla, or M &Ms to the cookies. This is true in writing your ACT essay as well. A few M & Ms will make it tastier, but don't forget the main ingredients like flour, baking soda and sugar -- the essentials.

Writing a really good ACT essay is really as simple as following a blueprint or a plan.

bold print: this is essential
regular print: this is a suggestion
italics: this is a sample sentence

Here is what's going to go into our Cheat Sheet

Title: <u>*Try, Try, and Try Again*</u>
(Technically a title is not a requirement, but it does help with focus. You can even recycle or modify the title from the essay prompt itself).

Introductory paragraph with
lead: Why not open with a question?
Can you imagine what America's Founding Fathers would think if they could see the United States of the 21st Century? **-or-**
Hook your reader in with an interesting quotation or idea.
My favorite teacher used to say that "A journey of a thousand miles begins with a single step." or
"A single word," I thought to myself, as I faced the daunting task of writing a whole book about the perfect ACT essay.

2-4 sentences that introduce the topic of the essay and the various perspectives.

thesis: wrap up the introductory paragraph with your thesis. A good thesis in standardized test writing often includes the word because. The word "because" tips the reader off to the fact that you are explaining the "why" of your opinion. It is essential to write a clear ACT thesis because letting your reader see your main idea at the end of the first paragraph makes it easy for him or her to give you a high score.
"The ACT is a valuable tool for quickly comparing students' abilities; however, <u>because</u> the test does have many shortcomings, it's best used in conjunction with GPA, personal statements, letters of recommendation, and other data."

body paragraph #1 starts with a
topic sentence: Your first sentence in the first body paragraph should start big. Is this going to be a financial, psychological, or environmental paragraph, or are you considering the pros and cons of one of the three perspectives?
"Some of the problems with the ACT become clear when we view the issue from a financial perspective."
4-8 sentences that deepen the discussion introduced in the topic sentence. Dig deep. Think about anything you've seen on the topic. Have you discussed this in class? Seen a newspaper headline? Is the topic explored in a documentary you have seen or a book you have read?

body paragraph #2 starts with a
transition to the new paragraph **with a new topic sentence:**
Liberals, on the other hand, have a very different idea about the role of government in individuals' lives **- or -**
Another useful way to consider this issue is from a financial perspective.
4-8 sentences that deepen the discussion. A good idea is to pop an authoritative source

into one of your body paragraphs.

In my AP US History class, we learned that - **or** -

I recently read in <u>the New York Times</u>... (underline book titles, magazines, & newspapers)

If you're using the "-al" structure, what's another relevant angle? Societal? Physical? If you're tackling this essay one perspective at a time, it's time to consider the next perspective.

body paragraph #3 starts with another

transition to the new paragraph **with a new topic sentence**.

Although the first two perspectives clearly have serious flaws, there is another perspective with much more promise - or -

Finally, one can consider this issue from the issue of security...

followed by

4-8 sentences that deepen the discussion.

Many students shy away from using "I" in these essays because a teacher has told them "Don't ever use 'I' in your essays for school." This is an exception. A personal anecdote, story or snapshot of your life is very convincing and compelling at the right moment. Pow!

The question of immigration hits home for me, especially, because when I was in the first grade, my uncle immigrated from Vietnam and came to live with us...

Conclusion: restate thesis, with a fresh "because" that wraps up all the '-als' you've used (or summarizes the three perspectives).

As you can see from the myriad financial, cultural, social and finally personal examples, it's clear that the best view on immigration is...because... - **or** -

Although some Americans believe that the government should serve as a 'nanny' in our lives and others think the government should leave us alone, the best approach is to seek a happy medium between these two extremes...

Reframe with a Big Bang ending:

In the United States, we see more and more...

In ten years, we can expect to see..

Around the world, in our technologically-connected, world-is-flat economy, it's easy to see that... - **or** -

alternatively, lower the volume, lean in and bring it down to a whisper by writing something narrow and personal for your last sentence.

For me, as I reflect on the last moments of my teenage years...

As high school is drawing to a close...

tear this page out and use it to outline (or download a copy from mightyoakgames.com/downloads.html)

ACT ESSAY CHEAT SHEET

Title:

lead:

thesis w/because:

body # 1: main idea (al?)

body # 2: main idea (source, quotation?)

body # 3: main idea (personal "I" story)

conclusion: restate thesis, "Big Bang" ending or a new story or small fact, proverb, wise saying

Recipe for a 36 score on the ACT essay includes all of these ingredients:

☐ has a clearly-stated position on the issue, easily found in thesis with the word 'because'
☐ addresses all 3 perspectives
☐ has a length of 3 + pages. Yes, 3 pages minimum, getting onto the 4th page is even better
☐ skips lines between paragraphs and indents(makes essay easier to read)
☐ has some flashy vocab that you're sure you are using properly

and should include 3 or more of these:

☐ a personal story using "I"
☐ a relevant study or news item
☐ something relevant you have learned in school

☐ is there a rhetorical question?
☐ a proverb or wise saying
☐ a direct quote

Did you say something about **flashy vocab?**
Yes. Remember that the "L" subscore on your essay reflects your use of Language.

So far, most of our tips have been about the main standardized parts of writing, which are Ideas and Organization. Now, where is that part we talked about earlier when we said that you--the writer--could improvise and customize ? The M & Ms ? The extra vanilla and spice?

It's in the style. Your writing style -- this is all you. You may think that you don't have a writing style, but you do. You have a voice, and now is a good time to think about what it is, especially if you have never done so. Are you a casual and friendly writer? This is how I write, for example, because my goal is to reach out to you in a simple and direct way and to make this topic (test taking), which is anxiety- and pressure-filled, less worrisome. Is your style going to be scholarly because you are a good student, or will it be like a reporter's style? I encourage you to write with color, precision and flair. Feel free to show off your personality and character in the flow of your sentences, albeit grammatically correct sentences. Can you have a paragraph that is a just a single word?

Yes.

That's wild, but it makes a strong point. Can you ask questions in the middle of your essay ?

Yes.

The grader has many, many essays to read, all on the same topic. Can you imagine how boring this would get after an hour or two, reading basically the same essay over and over, as your cup of herbal tea grows cold? Your legs fall asleep under the weight of the cat asleep on your lap, the TV is playing a game show in the background, that day-old blueberry bran muffin sits half-eaten on your vintage china plate, and you're in a hypnotic trance from the monotony of unremarkable essay after unremarkable essay. Spice it up! Give the grader a pleasant surprise with something colorful and well-crafted to enjoy.

Here are a few words and phrases that our best students have found helpful to punch up their essays.

verbs	nouns	etcetera * extras
illuminates	facet	consequently
clarifies	aspect	as a result
exaggerates	lens	especially key
passionately argues	approach	significantly
elucidates	dimension	irrefutably
demonstrates	counterpoint	compelling
emphasizes	element	convincing
illustrates	criterion	ostensibly
diminishes	correlation	discerning

Transitions

On the other hand

In contrast

The opposite side suggests

The other side of the coin is that

As a result

Moreover

One could argue

Some believe that, some argue

May I suggest

Consequently

At the other end of the spectrum

Furthermore

Wisdom from well-known sources:

Gandhi: "Live as if you were to die tomorrow. Learn as if you were to live forever."

Confucius: "It does not matter how slowly you go, as long as you don't stop."

MLK: "Intelligence plus character--that is the true goal of education."

Aristotle: "Knowing yourself is the beginning of all wisdom."

Socrates: "The only true wisdom is in knowing that you know nothing."

Oprah: "Turn your wounds into wisdom"

Churchill: "It is the courage to continue that counts"

Herman Melville: "It is better to fail at originality that to succeed at imitation."

Oscar Wilde: "We live in an age when unnecessary things are our only necessities."

"Be yourself, everybody else is taken."

Proverbs: common sense isn't so common, so <u>read and learn</u>, my young friends

Two wrongs don't make a right

Absence makes the heart grow fonder

All that glitters is not gold

Let sleeping dogs lie

Better late than never

Birds of a feather flock together

Don't judge a book by its cover

If at first you don't succeed, try and try again

No pain, no gain

A leopard cannot change its spots

Might makes right

Nothing hurts like the truth

Knowledge is power

The pen is mightier than the sword

Practice makes perfect

Knowledge is suffering

Rome wasn't built in a day

Variety is the spice of life

Too many cooks spoil the broth

Practice makes perfect: practice, practice, practice

Section 2: Twelve Essay Prompts
(and how to use them)

We have crafted these 12 essay prompts to reflect the themes that we believe are most likely to pop up on the ACT.

If you are reading this 4 weeks or more before your actual ACT:

--congratulations on your foresight! Make copies of the lined pages at the back of the book (or download pdfs from mightyoaktestprep.com/downloads.htm)

--set aside a 40-minute block of time

--set a timer for 40 minutes

--start your essay! Use the planning page to map out your essay, and then start writing.

--when your time is up (or the next day), review your essay. How was your pacing? How did the amount of time (40 minutes), amount of space (4 pages), amount of writing, and number of ideas all work out? If you ran out of ideas before the timer beeped, you should spend more time planning. If your essay was too short or too long, adjust your writing speed and/or the scope of your essay appropriately. Did your hand cramp? Mine too. It gets better. Practice makes perfect.

--Scrutinize your essay critically (or have a friend, parent, or teacher look at it). How were your Ideas? Development? Organization? Language and Grammar? If it were someone else's essay, would you want to read it? Does it flow well, make a logical argument, have great examples, and use colorful language and vocabulary? Reflect on what went well and what needs improvement, and then, a few days later, go do it all over again. Most people find that they get comfortable and confident with the ACT's essay structure after 2-4 tries. Don't give up -- persist until you're a master.

If you are reading this 1 or 2 weeks before the actual ACT:

--don't worry. You still have time to learn the fundamentals of ACT essay writing.

--follow the same steps as above on as many essays as you can (1-2 per week), and then outline the other topics until you feel like you have a good handle on what's expected.

If you are reading this the day before the test:

--we've all been there. Try not to get too anxious about it. Remember that the ACT is offered a half-dozen times a year and that you'll have many opportunities to succeed. If you don't get the score you want tomorrow, then sign up to take it again.

--look at the essay prompts and spend five minutes outlining each. Think about the big-picture issues involved, the key conflicts, and the views of each position. If you have the time, try writing one of the essays.

Struggles & Hardship

When many great people are asked to look back at their lives and identify the moments that defined their character, they typically recall struggles they endured and challenges they overcame. Indeed, many believe that struggle is the key component that drives personal growth. These people sometimes even seek out and embrace adversity for themselves and their loved ones. Others, however, recognize that struggles and challenges can be uncomfortable, unpleasant, unhealthy, and stressful, so they seek to avoid such hardships for themselves and their children.

Read and carefully consider these perspectives. Each suggests a particular way of thinking about the impact of struggles and hardship.

Perspective One	Perspective Two	Perspective Three
Without having challenges to overcome, we will never have the opportunity to discover what we are capable of achieving. Life without challenges makes people physically and mentally soft.	Our ancestors have toiled for centuries to create advances to make our lives easier. Why should we be forced to endure hardship? History and literature can teach us about hardship without our having to endure it personally.	School, sports, and activities provide us with ample opportunities to experience increasing levels of simulated hardship as we get older, helping to forge character and growth without forcing us to endure real deprivation or struggle.

Essay Task

Write a coherent, unified essay in which you evaluate multiple perspectives given on the subject of hardship. In your essay, be sure to:

> --analyze and evaluate the perspectives given
> --state and develop your own perspective on the issue
> --explain the relationship between your perspective and those given

Your perspective may be in full agreement with any of the others, in partial agreement, or wholly different. Whatever the case, support your ideas with logical reasoning and detailed, persuasive examples.

Immigration

The story of the United States is a story of immigration. From the very first settlers to recent waves of people fleeing strife in their native countries, the US is populated with people (or their ancestors) who originally called somewhere else home. Yet almost as long as there has been a United States, there has been disagreement about who should be allowed to immigrate, and several recent events have once again brought this issue to the forefront of public consciousness.

Read and carefully consider these perspectives. Each suggests a particular way of thinking about the impact of American immigration policies.

Perspective One	Perspective Two	Perspective Three
We are a nation of immigrants. With the exception of Native Americans, we (or our ancestors) are all immigrants to this country. It is hypocritical for us to deny others the same opportunity that we received by immigrating to this country. It is the obligation of our nation to welcome immigrants with open doors and open arms.	Immigrants are a potential resource to our nation, bringing a diversity of ideas, cultures, arts, and cuisines. Great thinkers and workers want to come to the USA, and foreigners at risk in their countries deserve asylum in ours. We should allow immigration if the immigrants can demonstrate that they will be contributors to (and not burdens on) our society.	Among those immigrating into this country are terrorists, drug dealers, rapists, and murderers. Immigrants take our jobs, driving up unemployment. Those who can't get jobs are forced to steal or sell drugs to survive, increasing crime. For the safety of ourselves and our children and the greater good of our nation, we must close our borders and deny further immigration.

Essay Task

Write a coherent, unified essay in which you evaluate multiple perspectives given on the impact of immigration. In your essay, be sure to:

--analyze and evaluate the perspectives given
--state and develop your own perspective on the issue
--explain the relationship between your perspective and those given

Your perspective may be in full agreement with any of the others, in partial agreement, or wholly different. Whatever the case, support your ideas with logical reasoning and detailed, persuasive examples.

High School Sports

Many high school students are encouraged to participate in sports at school. These programs, it is argued, teach students to work as part of a team, help to maintain physical fitness, make college applications more attractive, and can even lead to a lucrative professional sports career. However, participation often requires a time commitment of 12 hours or more per week, and some assert that this time could be better spent on academics and other activities. Furthermore, it is argued, academic courses teach broadly applicable skills that virtually every student will need for life after school; on the other hand, athletic activities seldom result in careers.

Read and carefully consider these perspectives. Each suggests a particular way of thinking about the role of sports in high school.

Perspective One	Perspective Two	Perspective Three
You're more likely to get a concussion than a career from high school sports. School is supposed to prepare you for college, career, and life, and playing on a sports team is of limited value in any of these areas.	The goal of high school is to create students who are stong in mind and in body. Our nation is becoming increasingly overweight and out of shape -- athletics are just as important as academics in high school to prepare students to make good choices after graduation.	Some students are good at books, and other students are good at sports. If a student finds athletics rewarding and academics a struggle, sports may be the only factor that keeps that student coming back to school every day.

Essay Task

Write a coherent, unified essay in which you evaluate multiple perspectives given on the subject of high school sports. In your essay, be sure to:

--analyze and evaluate the perspectives given
--state and develop your own perspective on the issue
--explain the relationship between your perspective and those given

Your perspective may be in full agreement with any of the others, in partial agreement, or wholly different. Whatever the case, support your ideas with logical reasoning and detailed, persuasive examples.

Civic Involvement

Since the founding of the United States, the nation has relied on citizens to be actively involved in government affairs -- as Lincoln reminded us in the Gettysburg Address, ours is a government "of the people, by the people, and for the people." Yet with each passing generation, the average citizen has increasingly removed him- or herself from participating in government.

Read and carefully consider these perspectives. Each suggests a particular way of thinking about the importance of civic involvement.

Perspective One	Perspective Two	Perspective Three
Our government works best when all citizens participate. Whether it's jury duty, campaigning for a candidate, reporting a broken streetlight, launching an initiative, or running for office, civic involvement ensures that government runs efficiently and fairly for all.	The point of a representative democracy like the one in the United States is that we elect passionate, trustworthy people to safeguard our interests. We have our own lives to live, whether as workers, as students, as parents or children, and we elect politicians to do the civic work for us.	Technology has made civic involvement almost unnecessary; news websites and social media continuously inform us of relevant local issues, keeping our politicians honest and making it trivially easy to let them know how we feel.

Essay Task

Write a coherent, unified essay in which you evaluate multiple perspectives given on the issue of civic involvement. In your essay, be sure to:

--analyze and evaluate the perspectives given
--state and develop your own perspective on the issue
--explain the relationship between your perspective and those given

Your perspective may be in full agreement with any of the others, in partial agreement, or wholly different. Whatever the case, support your ideas with logical reasoning and detailed, persuasive examples.

Minimum Wage

The "Income Gap" – the difference in earnings between the highest-paid and lowest-paid Americans – is at its highest level in decades. Some states have recently increased the minimum wage in an attempt to narrow this gap, and some politicians are suggesting a nationwide rise in the minimum wage. Supporters assert that this increase is necessary to ensure the average American has enough money to survive. Opponents of the measure, however, assert that the natural laws of supply and demand should set the minimum wage and that raising the minimum wage will make it more expensive for employers to hire workers. This will force employers to either hire fewer employees (leading to increased unemployment) or to raise the prices of their products (causing inflation, in which everything costs more, negating the effects of the higher wages).

Read and carefully consider these perspectives. Each suggests a particular way of thinking about the impact of minimum wage laws.

Perspective One	Perspective Two	Perspective Three
An increased minimum wage is common sense and is a great first step in helping to ensure all Americans have a minimum standard of living.	Increasing the minimum wage is likely to result in little real benefit to workers. Increased pay means higher costs for businesses, which will be passed along to consumers in the form of higher prices, negating any increase in income.	If you work hard and create value for your employer, you will be rewarded. Minimum wage laws discourage people from working hard because you get paid a minimum amount whether you work hard or not.

Essay Task

Write a coherent, unified essay in which you evaluate multiple perspectives given on the impact of minimum wage laws. In your essay, be sure to:

> --analyze and evaluate the perspectives given
> --state and develop your own perspective on the issue
> --explain the relationship between your perspective and those given

Your perspective may be in full agreement with any of the others, in partial agreement, or wholly different. Whatever the case, support your ideas with logical reasoning and detailed, persuasive examples.

Reaching Adulthood

In most states, people can start driving cars at the age of 16, but must wait until 18 to smoke, gamble, vote, and join the military. The national drinking age is even higher at 21. Some argue that this disparity makes little sense and that, for example, people old enough to smoke, gamble, and go to war should be able to drink alcohol as well.

Read and carefully consider these perspectives. Each suggests a particular way of thinking about the age of adulthood in America.

Perspective One

A car can be used as a 2-ton weapon of destruction. A person mature enough to drive a car is mature enough to vote, fight, and drink. The age of adulthood should be uniformly decreased to 16.

Perspective Two

The current system has evolved this way for a reason. For example, teens drive at 16 because they need the cars for work and school. Alcohol consumed by minors can affect brain development, so 21 makes sense for drinking.

Perspective Three

Today's teens are not adults, and in many ways are less mature than their predecessors. They can't drive without texting, lack the common sense to understand the health effects of smoking, and are ill-informed to vote. The age of adulthood for all of these activities should be raised to 21.

Essay Task

Write a coherent, unified essay in which you evaluate multiple perspectives given on the idea of adulthood. In your essay, be sure to:

--analyze and evaluate the perspectives given
--state and develop your own perspective on the issue
--explain the relationship between your perspective and those given

Your perspective may be in full agreement with any of the others, in partial agreement, or wholly different. Whatever the case, support your ideas with logical reasoning and detailed, persuasive examples.

Student Volunteering

Many high schools now require that their students volunteer to charities for a minimun number of hours per year. Schools argue that this idea has multiple benefits and few drawbacks: students learn to be good citizens and to help those in need, while organizations benefit in the form of free labor. Detractors, however, argue that the schools are primarily trying to pad students' resumes and that the requirement to volunteer could breed resentment.

Read and carefully consider these perspectives. Each suggests a particular way of thinking about the idea of student volunteering.

Perspective One	Perspective Two	Perspective Three
"Required volunteering" is an oxymoron. Forcing students to give their time is contrary to the spirit of volunteering. Students should WANT to help, not NEED to help, and many students' lives are already too crowded with academics and extracurriculars.	Giving students the opportunity to identify an area of need and then help out can be one of the most fulfilling achievements in a young person's life. People have become too self-centered, and this requirement will help remind people of the importance of volunteering after graduation as well.	Student volunteering is a ploy by high schools to make their college applicants look more attractive. An unskilled laborer spending a few token afternoons in a soup kitchen does little to really help the charity, to inspire the student, or to impress prospective colleges.

Essay Task

Write a coherent, unified essay in which you evaluate multiple perspectives given on the subject of student volunteering. In your essay, be sure to:

--analyze and evaluate the perspectives given
--state and develop your own perspective on the issue
--explain the relationship between your perspective and those given

Your perspective may be in full agreement with any of the others, in partial agreement, or wholly different. Whatever the case, support your ideas with logical reasoning and detailed, persuasive examples.

Individuality and conformity

History and literature are filled with stories of rugged individuals who become heroes by going their own way and ignoring the popular behavior, beliefs, and actions of their peers. On the other hand, we all live in a society where, as members of a community, we are expected to behave (and rewarded for behaving) like the other members of the community.

Read and carefully consider these perspectives. Each suggests a particular way of thinking about the notions of individuality and conformity.

Perspective One	Perspective Two	Perspective Three
Whether it's on a sports team, in a classroom, or at a workplace, acting like our peers is the best way to ensure the group operates smoothly. If we were to all act by our own set of rules, teams, workplaces, and classrooms would cease to function properly.	If individual members of society never thought differently, dressed differently, or acted differently, society would have no chance to progress. Most of our great breakthroughs have been achieved by people who were not afraid to be different from the crowd.	Individuality is like salt -- a small amount adds flavor to our lives, but too much ruins the whole dish. There is no problem with going against the crowd, assuming the defiant act is modest in scope and does not harm or damage others.

Essay Task

Write a coherent, unified essay in which you evaluate multiple perspectives given on the subject of individuality and conformity. In your essay, be sure to:

--analyze and evaluate the perspectives given
--state and develop your own perspective on the issue
--explain the relationship between your perspective and those given

Your perspective may be in full agreement with any of the others, in partial agreement, or wholly different. Whatever the case, support your ideas with logical reasoning and detailed, persuasive examples.

Social Media

Advances in technology have made the world smaller than ever. From a phone or computer, we can easily and inexpensively keep in constant contact with our family, friends, coworkers, and classmates via social media. But, say critics, being constantly connected comes with hidden costs and dangers. Physical bullying has given way to cyber-bullying. A constant stream of images from friends in exotic locations or with exciting people can lead us to fear that our own lives don't measure up. And, some assert, keeping up with friends and acquaintances online is no substitute for face-to-face interaction.

Read and carefully consider these perspectives. Each suggests a particular way of thinking about the impact of social media on our lives.

Perspective One	Perspective Two	Perspective Three
It's hard to imagine life before the rise of social media. Our phones and computers provide us with a constant stream of updates from our loved ones, even those in other states and countries, keeping us connected with those who are important to us and redefining the very idea of what it means to be part of a community.	Like most tools, social media can be helpful or harmful. If geography separates you from loved ones, social media can be invaluable for maintaining relationships. But if we're using social media to exaggerate our own experiences or we find ourselves turning to Facebook instead of a face-to-face conversation, it's time to reconsider our priorities.	"Social Media" is a misnomer. We have replaced face-to-face interactions with shallow snapshots of each others' lives, real conversations with 140 character blurbs and important news with updates on our friends' trivial activities.

Essay Task

Write a coherent, unified essay in which you evaluate multiple perspectives given on the subject of social media. In your essay, be sure to:

--analyze and evaluate the perspectives given
--state and develop your own perspective on the issue
--explain the relationship between your perspective and those given

Your perspective may be in full agreement with any of the others, in partial agreement, or wholly different. Whatever the case, support your ideas with logical reasoning and detailed, persuasive examples.

Free Speech on Campus

Colleges have traditionally been viewed as places where people -- students and faculty -- have been free to speak their minds. However, a new trend has been on the rise. Student protesters are targeting people, ideas, traditions, and even building names that they find hurtful or offensive. These protesters argue that college should be a "safe space" where they can be free to be themselves while they study and learn without feeling their beliefs or opinions are being attacked. The ideas of "free speech" and "safe space" have often clashed, triggering protests, hunger strikes, and faculty dismissals. Some professors argue that they can't possibly avoid offending everyone, that challenging beliefs is a big part of the college experience, and that to even attempt to sanitize their lectures amounts to censorship.

Read and carefully consider these perspectives. Each suggests a particular way of thinking about free speech on college campuses.

Perspective One	Perspective Two	Perspective Three
It's easy for wealthy white males to dismiss or resist demands for a safe space on campus because their ethnicity, values, and beliefs are seldom challenged. Attracting and retaining minority students is hard enough, and failing to provide a nurturing, non-threatening environment will perpetuate the problem.	Universities have been the birthplace of some of modern society's most radical ideas. If we are in constant fear of offending someone, we will self-censor our speech. The ability to freely discuss, debate, and challenge traditions and strongly-held beliefs is vital to the development of individuals and society.	The people at universities are supposed to be among the brightest minds in our nation, so they should have the common sense to not be intentionally offensive and to not be easily offended.

Essay Task

Write a coherent, unified essay in which you evaluate multiple perspectives given on the subject of free speech on campus. In your essay, be sure to:

--analyze and evaluate the perspectives given
--state and develop your own perspective on the issue
--explain the relationship between your perspective and those given

Your perspective may be in full agreement with any of the others, in partial agreement, or wholly different. Whatever the case, support your ideas with logical reasoning and detailed, persuasive examples.

Free Education

Free education from Kindergarten through 12th grade has long been a tradition in the United States, and many local and state governments now offer low-cost 2-year community colleges as well. Now, some politicians are proposing that free education be extended to include traditional 4-year colleges. Supporters argue that the cost of a college education has spiraled out of control and that those who most need higher education are those who can least afford it. Critics argue that we can't afford to fund colleges and that a diploma from a free public university will be perceived as being vastly inferior to one from a private school.

Read and carefully consider these perspectives. Each suggests a particular way of thinking about the impact of offfering free college education.

Perspective One	Perspective Two	Perspective Three
Our current free educational system is already of dubious value; extending this system to college merely adds additional expenses to an already overburdened government and will not result in a more educated population.	It is incumbent upon our society that we provide all residents with access to quality education, but we needn't provide it for free. People seldom value what is freely given, and students who truly want education will find a way to pay for it.	Education is an investment in our future; an educated population is a happy, prosperous population and any expenses generated by offering free education will be more than offset by an increase in tax revenues from this newly prosperous population.

Essay Task

Write a coherent, unified essay in which you evaluate multiple perspectives given on the subject of free college. In your essay, be sure to:

--analyze and evaluate the perspectives given
--state and develop your own perspective on the issue
--explain the relationship between your perspective and those given

Your perspective may be in full agreement with any of the others, in partial agreement, or wholly different. Whatever the case, support your ideas with logical reasoning and detailed, persuasive examples.

Society and Laws

All societies operate under a set of rules or laws that the members of the society agree to follow. But, as a member of a society, are you obligated to follow its laws even if those laws are unjust? Some argue that laws are made by humans, and humans are unlikely to be completely unbiased, so laws are not necessarily fair to all members of society. When these laws are unfair, these people, it is our obligation to challenge these unjust laws until they are changed.

Read and carefully consider these perspectives. Each suggests a particular way of thinking about society and laws.

Perspective One	Perspective Two	Perspective Three
Without laws, there is no such thing as a society -- there is anarchy. In a democracy, laws are passed only after going through a rigorous process to ensure they are fair and just. As a result, it is our obligation (to ensure the stability of our society) to obey and respect these laws.	Laws are not always fair, and are not always created for the benefit of the people. Martin Luther King Jr, Mahatma Gandhi, and Nelson Mandela all recognized that the laws were not fair, and knew that it was their duty to challenge the law to ensure fairness.	Whether everyone in a society thinks laws are "fair" or not is irrelevant. It is impossible to please every member of society, but we strive to create laws that are the most fair to the greatest number of people. If a law benefits the vast majority, then the few who are excluded should understand and not challenge the law.

Essay Task

Write a coherent, unified essay in which you evaluate multiple perspectives given on the subject of society and laws. In your essay, be sure to:

- --analyze and evaluate the perspectives given
- --state and develop your own perspective on the issue
- --explain the relationship between your perspective and those given

Your perspective may be in full agreement with any of the others, in partial agreement, or wholly different. Whatever the case, support your ideas with logical reasoning and detailed, persuasive examples.

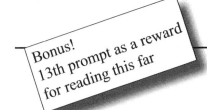
Bonus! 13th prompt as a reward for reading this far

Altruism vs Egoism

Each individual is a member of a society, and the actions of an individual have an effect on the society as a whole. Some people believe that, as members of a society, it's our obligation to help others in need without expecting anything in return. This idea is known as altruism. Others believe in egoism, the notion that each individual's striving to do what's best for him- or herself leads to the greatest overall benefit to society. Egoists assert that we know our own wants and needs better than anyone else does, so it is logical that we should all work to benefit ourselves. Offering help to others, egoists argue, is inefficient (because we can't perfectly know the wants or needs of others) and often degrading.

Read and carefully consider these perspectives. Each suggests a particular way of thinking about helping ourselves and others.

Perspective One	Perspective Two	Perspective Three
Our society is only as strong as its weakest member. Allowing others to suffer is unethical, and if we want to succeed and thrive as a society, it is our obligation to help the members of our society who are in need.	A sinking ship can't save another sinking ship. What is the point of trying to help another individual if we ourselves are in need? A society made up of people striving to help themselves be the best people they can be is the strongest society.	There is no such thing as true altruism. When people help others, they do so because they have been conditioned by others to give and because they experience feelings of satisfaction when they give. Being altruistic is motivated more by feeling good about ourselves than helping others.

Essay Task

Write a coherent, unified essay in which you evaluate multiple perspectives given on the subject of altruism and egoism. In your essay, be sure to:

--analyze and evaluate the perspectives given
--state and develop your own perspective on the issue
--explain the relationship between your perspective and those given

Your perspective may be in full agreement with any of the others, in partial agreement, or wholly different. Whatever the case, support your ideas with logical reasoning and detailed, persuasive examples.

Plan Your Essay Here
Writing on this page will not be used to determine your score
(but don't be tempted to just go to the next page and start writing – planning is crucial!)

Use the space below to plan your essay and come up with ideas. Here are some things to think about:

Consider the strengths and weaknesses of the three provided perspectives
   –do they make useful points? What are they forgetting to think about?
   –why might they be convincing or unconvincing to other people?

Personal experiences, beliefs, and knowledge
   –what is your personal position on this topic? What are the strong and weak points of your position?
   –how will you compellingly argue for this position in your essay?

On the real test, you will get one page (like the previous page) to outline your essay and four pages to write it. We have included these pages to let you know exactly how much space you will have on test day. Using lined paper for your practice essays is okay, but it's even better if you tear out and make copies of these five pages to be more accurate.

And yes, the first page of the essay really is shorter than the rest. On the real test, this space will have slots where you fill in your test booklet and writing test form numbers. This page is seven lines shorter than the next three.

Start the WRITING TEST here.

_____

_____

_____

_____

_____

_____

_____

_____

_____

_____

_____

_____

_____

_____

_____

_____

_____

_____

If you are not done, please continue on the next page.

WRITING TEST

_____

_____

_____

_____

_____

_____

_____

_____

_____

_____

_____

_____

_____

_____

_____

_____

_____

_____

_____

_____

_____

_____

_____

_____

_____

_____

If you are not done, please continue on the next page.

WRITING TEST

_____

_____

_____

_____

_____

_____

_____

_____

_____

_____

_____

_____

_____

_____

_____

_____

_____

_____

_____

_____

_____

_____

_____

_____

_____

If you are not done, please continue on the next page.

WRITING TEST

_____

_____

_____

_____

_____

_____

_____

_____

_____

_____

_____

_____

_____

_____

_____

_____

_____

_____

_____

_____

_____

_____

_____

_____

_____

_____

_____

STOP the Writing Test.

Made in the USA
Lexington, KY
19 March 2017